Committed

A daily devotional guide for those serious about taking this thing called Christianity and making it look like the Bible definition.

Donnie Clark

Copyright 2015 Donnie Clark

All rights reserved. No portion of this book may be reproduced, stored in a retrieval system, or transmitted, in any form or by any means – mechanical, photocopying, recording, or otherwise – without prior written permission of Donnie Clark.

"If you do not plan to live the Christian life totally committed to knowing your God and to walking in obedience to Him, then don't begin, for this is what Christianity is all about. It is a change of citizenship, a change of governments, and a change of allegiance. If you have no intention of letting Christ rule your life, then forget Christianity; it is not for you..."
Kay Arthur

Dedicated to the Nazirites, the committed, the remnants, the ones who know there is more and are willing to consecrate to have it! May this further fan your fire!

Index:

Day 1: The basics: prayer – *understanding prayer, and how to make it effective in the life of the committed*

Day 2: The basics: fasting – *the most disobeyed command in all the Bible*

Day 3: The basics: giving – *All the church wants is my money*

Day 4: Kingdom Community – *How God designed His Church*

Day 5: The power of Spiritual Authority- *You weren't meant to be a Lone Ranger*

Day 6: Why Christians Quit – *Recognizing patterns that will pull you away and removing them*

Day 7: Invading This Babylon – *Taking this thing outside of the Church walls ...*

This is NOT elementary. This is intense.

There will be a lot of meditation involved in this devotion...

If you are not willing to commit, stop now...

There will be a lot of writing, and things to memorize....

Once you turn this page, you'll be taking a journey that few are willing to take.

Therefore you will need a pen.... A Bible and a highlighter!

You have full permission to quote this book on social media to help spread the word that there is material out there to help you stay the course of the committed!! So do it!

Chapter 1

"The basics: prayer"

In the Bible they prayed and miracles happened, chains fell off, doors opened, the dead were raised, foundations shook, masses were converted. We pray and nothing happens. Period. Something has to change.

To understand the Kingdom of God, you must understand this key principle:

> "If the pursuit never stops, the discovery never ends."

Matthew 5:8 (Write it down): *Blessed are the pure in heart: for they shall see God.*

The "Pure in heart" get to see God... What in the world does that mean? Is that a "now" thing, or a "when I get to Heaven" thing? Understand that the

Kingdom is a "now" thing. And in order to "see God" now, you have to get into His Kingdom, because He is sitting on His throne. And to get into His Kingdom you have to ascend unto the hill of the Lord...

Psalm 24:3-6 (NIV)

Who may ascend the hill of the LORD ? Who may stand in his holy place? He who has **clean hands and a pure heart,** *who does not lift up his soul to an idol or swear by what is false He will receive blessing from the LORD and vindication from God his Savior. Such is the generation of those who seek him, who seek your face, O God of Jacob.*

It didn't say, "Those who attend Church". It didn't say, "Those who feel bad about their sin". It didn't say, "Those who are too busy can still see Me". It said, "Those with clean hands and pure hearts".

And after Jesus was purified in the Desert, all that was left of Him was the Kingdom... He was seeing God, because He was pure in heart.

When you see God, you see His Kingdom, and His heart for the earth is to manifest His kingdom.

Jesus explains that there are 3 characteristics of Kingdom people in Matthew 6.

Stop now and read Matthew 6:1-18

Write the three "when you" statements: _When you give, when you pray, when you fast_

These are character traits of the committed! When Jesus says, "when you fast", He is describing what committed people do, and trying to show you that fasting connects you to His presence. Your spirit is the only thing capable of being in His presence. And a denial of flesh that allows your Spirit to be in control. When Jesus says, "When you give", He is describing the natural character of the committed. Because giving of yourself is a denial of what you want, and allows you to be a part of building His kingdom. Money, time, Study of the word, etc.

Our lifestyle becomes that of the Kingdom when we regularly practice these three things; fasting, giving, and prayer.

Do you practice these three things consistently? _not enough_

What is keeping you from being consistent in these areas? _business, laziness_

Today's topic of study is prayer as it relates to Kingdom effectiveness. I want you to read along in your Bible. Your version may say something a little different but you will get the idea.

Read Matthew 6:5-13 again…

What is your definition of a hypocrite??? _Someone whose words & actions do not line up as the same_

Hypocrites are people whose lifestyle does not line up with their statement about themselves. They do not do what they say they do.

Some people who love to pray simply do it so that people will notice them and think they are right with God, but display of prayer, without a heart centered on God does not constitute rightness with God. They are hypocrites. That is not meant to insult them; it just is what it is. Many of us are hypocritical at times in our lives. That's not a dig, it just happens.

Other people only pray when they are at church simply because they are lazy, and don't make time for it, or see it as important. They are hypocrites also. It is not meant to offend, it is simply fact. Some people pray, as a ritualistic, legalistic response to feel good about their "works".

What I want to get to is the root of your reasoning for prayer. Are you genuinely focused and connected every time you pray? __yes (room for improvement)__ Is your prayer specific and true and heartfelt every time?? __yes when purposefully done, scattered when it's forced__ Do you ever examine yourself and see that you are hypocritical at times? __yes__

These need to be honest answers. You'll never really commit until you *admit* that there's a deficiency in your prayer life.

Next, Jesus addresses a problem of getting into a routine of meaningless words:

Verse 7 – "And when you pray, do not use vain <u>repetitions</u> as the heathen do. For they think that they will be heard for their many words."

Showing us that our prayers should have meaning to them. That we need to understand the power of our words. But for many of us, it's easy to get into this routine of repetitive words. So, it's important to recognize in yourself that when you are just saying things that are common, you have entered into a prayer that is ineffective, and at best, just gets you heard by other people...

<u>Listen to how you pray</u>. Say a quick prayer that is your normal language of prayer, and listen to the meaningless words you use because that's how you've been taught to pray... Do you think God is moved by how many times you say, "Father", or "Dear Jesus", or whatever your catch phrase is???

_____

Is that how you talk to your mother?? Do you say, "Dearest mother, I ask thee, oh wonderful mother, that if thou wilst, oh precious mother, please allow me, dear mother, to feel your love, oh gracious mother"??? Think about it... But that's how many of us pray to God.

He's not impressed

Your prayer has to have meaning and heart if it's going to make a difference on earth as it is being done in heaven... And Jesus gives us a guideline of how to pray effectively for Kingdom results...

1.) Recognize the importance of identification of who God is in prayer

"In this manner, therefore, pray: Our Father in heaven,"

This is a statement of direct identification to relationship. To understand proper identification, you need to understand the power of your words: that when you speak in alignment with Kingdom, ✷ you allow The Father to force dominion in your life.

Luke 1:38 (write it down): And Mary said, Behold the handmaid of the Lord, be it unto me according to thy word. And the angel departed from her.

"So the Word became human and made his home among us."

John 1:14

The power of your words aligning with God's will is vital in understanding Kingdom praying. And Jesus teaches Kingdom people to be sure to identify immediately who you are praying to. Why do you think He would do such a thing? Why is it important in identifying who exactly you are praying to? Because of the many gods or idols set before us, it is good to specify who our God is

He does this because of the great power of our words. When you begin your prayers out with the statement, "God...", or "Lord", then, because of the power of the spoken word, you are immediately praying to whatever it is that is god in your life! You are praying to whatever it is that is Lord in your life. So, if your god for the day is Facebook, then Facebook is not going to answer your prayer, but that's who you are praying to! If your god is your boyfriend/girlfriend or spouse, then walking into your prayer closet and praying to "god" is not going to get you anywhere.

So, it's important for <mark>Kingdom prayers to be done with a specific identification of who our Lord and Father really are</mark>. Jesus specifically said, "<u>Our Father, in Heaven.</u>" This is deep because He is <u>directly identifying</u> <u>the one true Living God who dwells in Heaven as His Father!</u>

Look up these scriptures, write them down:

Deuteronomy 10:20: _Thou shalt fear the Lord thy God; Him shalt thou serve, and to Him thou shalt cleave, and swear by His name_

Psalm 9:10: _And they that know thy name will put their trust in thee: for thou, Lord, hast not forsaken them that seek thee_

Proverbs 18:10: _The name of the Lord is a strong tower: the righteous runneth into it, and is safe._

Joel 2:32: _And it shall come to pass, that whosoever shall call on the name of the Lord shall be delivered_

Did you know that His name is not God? That is His title! He is God! But that's not His name! Just a few of the names found in Scripture for Him are "Elohim", which means "Creator, mighty and Strong". Another name found is "Adonai", which means "Lord"! He is called "Yahweh", which strictly speaking, is the only proper name for God. Translated in English Bibles "LORD" (all capitals) to distinguish it from Adonai "Lord." This is the revelation of the name first given to Moses when He says, "I Am who I Am"…

He wants you to understand that He is your Father. He wants you to identify with Him as someone who loves you! Someone who cares about what you accomplish, and what you believe, and how you end up and who you marry! He is a real Father! He is not some un-approachable figure.

Kingdom prayer is effective when we understand that we are not praying to some god who is sitting somewhere on a throne who does not care. We are talking to our Father!

2.) Hallowed be thy Name

He is Holy Father, but an idea of God as Father, without Hallowed be thy name creates a disrespect for Him. There should be a holy righteous reverence for God balanced with Him being Father! Effective Kingdom praying places a Holy fear and respect on God for who He is to you. He is not your *homeboy*, the *big guy in the sky*, or the *man upstairs*. He is the God of all creation, and that demands reverence!

Why does this generation not respect God? It's very likely that it is because their home example of a father does not demand respect. Most don't have a father that exemplifies what a father should be, and, by default, they are not able to learn how to properly honor authority figures.

The word *hallowed* literally means, - "To be held in reverence". The word phrase, "Thy Name" indicated not just His name, but the entirety of the person's character, their attributes, and heart that is revealed through their name. That is a lot more than just *"the name"*! When you pray Kingdom prayers, you are putting reverence onto the Character of Christ!

Psalm 34:3 (write it down):_____

_____

_____

3.) His will

Verse 10 - *Your kingdom come.* ***Your will*** *be done on earth as it is in heaven.*

In order for you to produce the King's dominion, you must be willing to be the channel through which the king can manifest His will. Your mind and your body can't comprehend the kingdom, but your spirit can. That's why you **must be willing to deny yourself what it wants to produce the thoughts of Heaven** in the Earth.

His will is to make Earth look like Heaven... But what does that look like? In Heaven sickness can't exist, and He wants *YOU* to bring that Kingdom into this world! He wants to use you as a channel that when sick people get around you, they can't stay sick anymore!! In Heaven, there are no addictions to drugs, alcohol, pornography, and the like, but you don't have to wait until you get to Heaven to be free of those! Your prayers bring that Kingdom here! And God wants to use you as a channel that when people with addictions get around you, they won't know how or why, but those addictions will be pulled out of them and the thing that used to grip them, now disgusts them! In Heaven, you exist to bring honor to God in all you do! So God's will is that you be a channel to where everything you do brings honor to Him here, and now! That's why it is hypocritical for you to cry and snot and worship God in church, and disobey your parents! That's why you can't just come into church and jump and holler, and pray, but won't make your bed!

His ultimate will is that His Sons and Daughters represent His name well. How you act is a direct reflection of His influence over you! If you're always negative, disrespectful, angry, broke, sick; then you are not representing Him well, and that's not His will for you!

What is God's will?

John 6:40 (write it down): _____

_____

_____

Read the following slowly, and highlight what you feel is important to you!!

Ephesians 5:8-17 NKJV

For you were once darkness, but now *you are* light in the Lord. Walk as children of light (for the fruit of the Spirit *is* in all goodness, righteousness, and truth), finding out what is acceptable to the Lord. And have no fellowship with the unfruitful works of darkness, but rather expose *them*. For it is shameful even to speak of those things which are done by them in secret. But all things that are exposed are made manifest by the light, for whatever makes manifest is light. Therefore He says: " Awake, you who sleep, Arise from the dead, And Christ will give you light." See then that you walk circumspectly, not as fools but as wise, redeeming the time, because the days are evil. Therefore do not be unwise, but understand what the <u>will of the Lord</u> *is*.

1 Thessalonians 5:11-18 NKJV

    Therefore comfort each other and edify one another, just as you also are doing. And we urge you, brethren, to recognize those who labor among you, and are over you in the Lord and admonish you, and to esteem them very highly in love for their work's sake. Be at peace among yourselves. Now we exhort you, brethren, warn those who are unruly, comfort the fainthearted, uphold the weak, be patient with all. See that no one renders evil for evil to anyone, but always pursue what is good both for yourselves and for all. Rejoice always, pray without ceasing, in everything give thanks; for <u>this is the will of God</u> in Christ Jesus for you

According to just these few scriptures, list in your own words, what you think the will of God is, that you should be praying, and walking in?_____

_____

_____

_____

_____

_____

All of this is part of YOUR prayer life!!!

4.) Give us this day our daily bread

This is self-explanatory; don't get ahead of God...

You can't offer something to people that you don't possess! Don't preach about sin when you're bound by it. Don't talk about the authority of God if you're not walking in it. Don't talk about healing if you're not healing people. Don't talk about being free if you're still bound by lust!

So, your prayer should be, whatever you have for me today, I want it! I can't handle what's up the road, so I need to chew on what you have for me now!

If we do not understand this, then we never learn how to accept what God has for us today, so we never tap into what He has for us in a week from now, and we never do anything of importance!

Foundations are never seen!!! Have you ever seen the concrete under your floor??? But if it were not there, your house would fall! And you can't build walls without a proper foundation! This is the foundation to living the committed life! Effective praying!

5.) <u>Forgive us our debts as we forgive our debtors</u>

Romans 2:1-2 (write it down):_____

_____

_____

_____

_____

Matthew 7:1-2 (write it down):_____

_____

_____

Matthew 18:21-35 NKJV

Then Peter came to Him and said, "Lord, how often shall my brother sin against me, and I forgive him? Up to seven times?" Jesus said to him, "I do not say to you, up to seven times, but up to seventy times seven. Therefore the kingdom of heaven is like a certain king who wanted to settle accounts with his servants. And when he had begun to settle accounts, one was brought to him who owed him ten thousand talents. But as he was not able to pay, his master commanded that he be sold, with his wife and children and all that he had, and that payment be made. The servant therefore fell down before him, saying, 'Master, have patience with me, and I will pay you all.' Then the master of that servant was moved with compassion, released him, and forgave him the debt. "But that servant went out and found one of his fellow servants who owed him a hundred denarii; and he laid hands on him and took *him* by the throat, saying, 'Pay me what you owe!' So his fellow servant fell down at his feet and begged him, saying, 'Have patience with me, and I will pay you all.' And he would not, but went and threw him into prison till he should pay the debt. So when his fellow servants saw what had been done, they were very grieved, and came and told their master all that had been done. Then his master, after he had called him, said to him, 'You wicked servant! I forgave you all that debt because you begged me. Should you not also have had compassion on your fellow servant, just as I had pity on you?' And his master was angry, and delivered him to the torturers until he should pay all that was due to him. "So My heavenly Father also will do to you if each of you, from his heart, does not forgive his brother his trespasses."

Why do you think God is so adamant about you walking in forgiveness? _____
_____

What areas of your life (people, issues, hurts) do you struggle with forgiveness? _____
_____
_____

6.) <u>And lead us not into temptation</u>

Why in the World would Jesus pray this in His prayer? Knowing that Jesus had the full revelation of who God is. Knowing the Kingdom, knowing the will of God. Why pray this? He says this as to almost insinuate that God has the capability to lead you into temptation.

But James 1:13-14 says that *"When tempted, no one should say, "God is tempting me." For God cannot be tempted by evil, nor does he tempt anyone; but each one is tempted when, by his own evil desire, he is dragged away and enticed."*

Here's a principle that you need to really understand:

"Trials come from God… Temptations come from Satan."

So why add this to your prayer??? Jesus is clear to show us that we are to recognize that everywhere God is leading us; the enemy will be there to tempt us! Everywhere God is leading you; Satan will be there to tempt you. And the only way you can understand the truth of this kind of praying is to have first spent time following God's leading into a wilderness…

Mark 1:12-13 (write it down): _____

_____

_____

What He's saying is, "I'm following You, make sure where you lead me, I can't fail..."

1 Corinthians 10:13 (NLT)

The temptations in your life are no different from what others experience. And God is faithful. He will not allow the temptation to be more than you can stand. When you are tempted, he will show you a way out so that you can endure.

(You should have highlighted that like crazy!!!)

Today, as you close out this devotion, take a few moments and write down some hindrances that are in your life that you need to deal with. Write down some areas you are committing to change. Write down things you want to see happen in your community, and then commit to seeing them happen because you are a Kingdom praying Son or daughter._____

_____

_____

_____

_____

_____

Chapter 2

"The basics: fasting"

The most disobeyed command in all of the Bible

The three characters of Kingdom people are prayer, fasting, and giving. Character is defined as: "the set of qualities that make somebody or something distinctive, qualities that make somebody or something interesting or attractive!" So, if you want

Matthew 6:1-18 (read it again)

Again, we have three characteristics of Kingdom people, which is important because of what the scripture teaches about the number 3.

Ecclesiastes 4:12: _____

_____

That when Jesus said in Mark 4, "…a crop that sprang up, increased and produced: some thirtyfold, some sixty, and some a hundred." I teach that when you pray, you release a thirty fold blessing. Prayer with a giving heart releases sixty fold, and when all three are a part of your normal life, you release a hundred times the blessing that you invest in others, and in ministry!

Fasting must become a characteristic of what we are recognized by, therefore it must move from a discipline in your life to a natural byproduct of your pursuit of God's plan.

Fasting in scripture has been the secret to open doors, miraculous provision, favor, healings, miracles, deliverance and freedom! And our unwillingness to pursue it is a heresy in light of the scriptures and in comparison to the millions who have burned in the fire of true hunger, and seen the fruit of a true consecrated life.

Let's break fasting down:

1. **<u>What is fasting?</u>**

Well, fasting is not just going without food. That is dieting. Or possibly starving for some of us! Fasting is not sitting in front of the TV or skipping lunch break and working through lunch because you're not eating. That is starvation!

In the Bible, fasting is going without food for a spiritual purpose! Its purpose is to solely bring us into a deeper, more intimate relationship with God. It produces great power, but that cannot be why you fast. It keeps your focus on God, but that cannot be your reasoning for fasting. You MUST want inside of you so much to be more intimate with Him, and that's why you fast.

Psalm 42:1-3 NKJV

¹ As the deer pants for the water brooks, so pants my soul for You, O God. ² My soul thirsts for God, for the living God. When shall I come and appear before God? ³ My tears have been my food day and night,

Remember, if this doesn't mean anything to you, it's pointless. And fasting does nothing to change God! He cannot change! You're doing this for you!

Have you ever fasted? _____

Did you do it with the right understanding? _____

Do you see the purpose of fasting? _____

2. Is my not engaging in fasting a sin?

James 4:17 – if you know the good you ought to do, and do not do it, to him, it is a sin.

Revelation brings responsibility to steward over. Fasting was a part of everyday life in the Old Testament, and also in the New Testament! Just like giving, fasting has a basic expectation, and whatever you do above the expectation is only going to benefit you more. It is a command from Jesus. It is not open to your conviction.

Ezekiel 16:49-50

[49] Look, this was the iniquity of your sister Sodom: She and her daughter had pride, fullness of food, and abundance of idleness; neither did she strengthen the hand of the poor and needy. [50] And they were haughty and committed abomination before Me; therefore I took them away as I saw fit.

Many think of Sodom as being perverse, and it was, but the root of its sin was described here as "No giving" (poor and needy), "No praying" (pride and idleness), and they were guilty of gluttony (fullness of food)! This disobedience spiraled into the perversion of an entire city moving into homosexuality. But it started with disobedience to the commands of God. Esau lost his birthright to father the Nation because he had no control over his fleshly desire!

It's a command! It keeps your spirit dominant!

After reading this, would you agree that fasting is a Biblical command for Kingdom people?_____

Corporate fasting for the body:

Luke 6:40: _____

_____

_____

_____

If you are a part, then you go with the body.

1 Corinthians 12:20-26 NKJV

²⁰ But now indeed there are many members, yet one body. ²¹ And the eye cannot say to the hand, "I have no need of you"; nor again the head to the feet, "I have no need of you." ²² No, much rather, those members of the body which seem to be weaker are necessary. ²³ And those members of the body which we think to be less honorable, on these we bestow greater honor; and our unpresentable parts have greater modesty, ²⁴ but our presentable parts have no need. But God composed the body, having given greater honor to that part which lacks it, ²⁵ that there should be no schism in the body, but that the members should have the same care for one another. ²⁶ And if one member suffers, all the members suffer with it; or if one member is honored, all the members rejoice with it.

If the pastor calls for a corporate fast, you do it!

<u>Individual fasting:</u>

In the first church, they didn't have the New Testament, they were writing it! But they did have some writings that they adhered to! It was called *The Didache* or Teaching of the Apostles. It can be found online, but it does address fasting in Chapter 8, verses 1 & 2:

And let not your fastings be with the hypocrites, for they fast on the second and the fifth day of the week; 8:2 but do ye keep your fast on the fourth and on the preparation (the sixth) day.

So individual fasting was done two days a week, every week, their entire lives. Matthew Henry (wrote the commentary of the Bible) says, "Those who are under the power of a carnal mind will have their lusts fulfilled, though it be to the certain damage and ruin of their precious souls."

Romans 6:14 – sin is no longer your master

Proverbs 25:28: _____

_____

_____

1 Corinthians 9:27: _____

_____

_____

_____

3. What kinds of fasts are Biblical?

Biblically, fasting is abstaining from food. Cutting out television is self-control, and it needs to happen, but it's not fasting. Cutting out chocolate, or "fasting" from gossip is not fasting. It's called growing up. Maturing... and it needs to happen!

Biblically, fasting is only associated with food. Medically, some people must take medication and need to take it with food. Your heart positioned correctly helps determine what is necessary and what it moved to excessive.

In the Bible, there are three types of fasts: An absolute fast, a normal fast and a partial fast.

An absolute fast is extreme and should be done only for short periods of time. It involves taking in nothing: no food, no water, nothing. It should be done with medical supervision. A normal fast is going without anything that is food. When doing this, you should drink plenty of water, chicken broth, etc. On a long fast, I will even have a milkshake or a smoothie to replenish my energy. Again, it's a heart thing. Putting fruit, cookies or steak into a blender is not acceptable. If you are willing to compromise in this, you have moved from a spiritual awakening into starving yourself for no purpose. Partial fasts are not what you do every night while you sleep. It involves giving up food and drink for a certain time frame. The most common example is the Daniel fast. Daniel fasted, taking in no sweets, no meat, and no wine for three weeks.

4. How often and how long should I fast?

In our busy lives there is always a holiday, birthday, office lunch, or something that creates a bump in the road, so we talk ourselves out of our fast. Corporately, we should fast together every beginning of a new year, and the reason why is that by doing so, you set the course for the rest of the year. Just like how you are beginning your day with prayer, you set the course for the rest of the day, and cover the things that happen next. Secondly, blessing will happen for you and your family throughout the year because you fasted in January. That's the law of first fruits! Abel offered the best of his first fruits! All throughout the year blessings will be finding their way to you because you sacrificed at the beginning of the year. Thirdly, when you fast at the beginning of the year, and pray... you release the principle found in Matthew 6:33, which says, "seek FIRST the kingdom of God and His righteousness, and all these things shall be added to you."

Individually, according to the Didache, fasting should be done two days a week, whether a normal fast, Daniel fast or absolute fast.

How long:

The duration of fasts vary. Biblically, there are significant numbers associated to fasts; three days, seven days, twenty-one days & forty days. You may feel the Lord call you to a daylight fast on Sundays for the church services. You may feel the Lord calling you to fast all beverages except water, as a prophetic gesture of His water to wash and purify our community.

My advice:

Outside of the Biblical assignment to fast two days a week and the corporate assignments given periodically, I would suggest you feel the prompting of Holy Spirit, submit it to spiritual authority for direction, and accountability, and you pursue God with all your guts. Go into a fast slowly. Don't gorge yourself the day before; it will cause your body to freak out the first day of fasting. Start slowing down on your eating knowing a fast is coming. Come out of it slowly. After three days, your digestive system takes a much needed break. So, to awaken it again, you come off the fast slowly. Start with a small bowl of soup, or some crackers, and just a few to awaken your senses again. Don't eat a full fledge meal until after you've snacked a full day after your fast has ended. Be prepared for the overflow…! It will come!

5. What does fasting accomplish; spiritual and physical?

Spiritually, fasting unlocks the power to walk in authority and manifest the character of the Kingdom through your spirit dominion over your flesh. Matthew tells us a story of a father who brought his boy to Jesus who had a demon. For years the father has watched this demon cause his son to suffer with severe convulsions. As the boy grew, the demon would throw the boy into fire and into water. The father brings the boy to the disciples and they could do nothing to remove the demon from the boy.

Matthew 17:18-21 KJV

[18]And Jesus rebuked the devil; and he departed out of him: and the child was cured from that very hour. [19] Then came the disciples to Jesus apart, and said, why could not we cast him out? [20] And Jesus said unto them, Because of your unbelief: for verily I say unto you, If ye have faith as a grain of mustard seed, ye shall say unto this mountain, Remove hence to yonder place; and it shall remove; and nothing shall be impossible unto you. [21] Howbeit this kind goeth not out but by prayer and fasting.

If you understand chronology, Jesus had already equipped the disciples and given them power to cast out evil spirits and to heal every disease. So, why couldn't the disciples cast out the demon and cure the boy? They wanted to know the same thing. Jesus said, "because of your unbelief". Jesus told them that they needed faith, but not only faith. Long before this incident, Jesus was led into the wilderness for forty days of fasting and prayer and equipping. And for Jesus… casting out a demon was not impossible. Because fasting had positioned him to walk in authority over his own flesh. And there is no way God will allow you to control demonic activity over other people when you cannot take control over your own flesh.

Fasting positions you to break the power of Satan to withhold God's plan and blessing. In Daniel 10, Daniel was grieved and burdened with the revelation he had received for Israel. He ate no choice breads or meats and drank no wine for three weeks. Then he describes the angel that was sent to him – which had been delayed by the Prince of Persia for twenty one days – with the answers Daniel sought after. Daniel's burden for others pushed him to fast, and this fast broke the power of the delayer and released the angels of God so that God's purpose could be revealed and served.

Physically, fasting is like a spring cleaning for your body. The first day of fasting, you should have one goal, and that is to consume at least one gallon of purified water throughout the day. Tap water does have impurities, so get a jug of purified water. Purified water helps flush out the toxins and the poisons in your system. And it will also aid in you feeling like you're full. That's important the first two days.

Have you ever had a headache when they tried fasting? It is not the Devil giving you the headache. It's actually a chemical issue. The headache in a fast is an indication that you really truly needed to fast. It is a result of the impurities and the poisons the body is burning for energy. These headaches stop completely after about two and a half to three days.

Tests have proven that the average American consumes and assimilates four pounds of chemical preservatives, coloring, stabilizers, flavorings, and other additives, each and every year of their life. These build up and cause illness and disease. Fasting gives your digestive system a break and gives your body the necessary time to heal itself of these toxins.

Keep drinking plenty of water and juice, and your body will flush itself out, and after the third day, you'll find that sweet place. That sweet place is the moment where your body has relinquished control to your spirit, and you will begin to sense a much deeper knowledge of God than you've ever thought possible.

Fasting has been proven to lower blood pressure and cholesterol! Don Colbert, MD, said, "Fasting does not only prevent sickness. If done correctly, fasting holds amazing healing benefits to those of us who suffer illness and disease. From colds, to flu's, to heart disease, fasting is a mighty key to healing the body."

Dr. Oda H.F. Birchinger said, "fasting can heal and help rheumatism in the joints and muscles, disease of the heart, circulation, blood vessels, stress-related exhaustion, skin diseases – including pimples and complexion problems, irregular menstrual cycles and hot flashes, hay fever, and even eye diseases."

To test the results of fasting on a human body, Dr. Tanner, another medical doctor decided at the age of fifty to fast forty three days without food under strict medical supervision. At the conclusion, he was extremely healthier than before. At age sixty, he fasted fifty days, and in the middle of his fast, records that he saw the unspeakable glories of God. At age 77, Dr. Tanner fasted fifty-three days, and besides the glorious spiritual awakenings, his once thin, gray hair was replaced with thick black hair. The same as in his youth. He also lived to be 93 years old.

Fasting slows your aging process. It allows the body to rest.

Deuteronomy 34:7: _____

_____

_____

Physically, fasting breaks our addiction to junk food and food in general. It can break addictions to nicotine, alcohol and even drugs. Fasting stirs a hunger inside of us, and a dull yearning that cannot allow us to rest. It pushes us to pursue Him, and that's what he wants!

Today, as you close out this devotion, take a few moments and pray and write down some commitments to fasting that you are making. And come back later and write the changes you are seeing!

_____

_____

_____

_____

_____

_____

_____

_____

_____

_____

_____

_____

_____

Chapter 3

"The basics: giving"

All the church wants is my money

That's simply not true. And that statement comes from a seed of greed anyway. If the three characters of Kingdom people are prayer, fasting, and giving, you cannot skip any of them! And giving is AS BIBLICALLY a Command as praying and fasting according to Jesus, and just as spiritual.

Malachi 3: 6-18 NKJV
"For I *am* the Lord, I do not change; therefore you are not consumed, O sons of Jacob. 7 Yet from the days of your fathers **you have gone away from my ordinances and have not kept** *them*. Return to Me, and I will return to you," says the Lord of hosts. "But you said, 'In what way shall we return?' 8 "Will a man rob God? Yet you have robbed Me! But you say, 'In what way have we robbed You?' **In tithes and offerings. 9 You are cursed with a curse, for you have robbed Me,** *even* this whole nation. 10 Bring **all the tithes into the storehouse**, that there may be food in My house, and try Me now in this," says the Lord of hosts, "If I will not open for you the

windows of heaven and pour out for you *such blessing that there will* not *be room* enough *to receive it.* ¹¹ **"And I will rebuke the devourer for your sakes, so that he will not destroy the fruit of your ground, nor shall the vine fail to bear fruit for you in the field,"** says the LORD of hosts; ¹² "And all nations will call you **blessed,** for you will be a delightful land," says the LORD of hosts. ¹³ "Your words have been harsh against Me," Says the LORD, "Yet you say, 'What have we spoken against You?' ¹⁴ You have said, 'It is useless to serve God; what profit *is it* that we have kept His ordinance, and that we have walked as mourners before the LORD of hosts? ¹⁵ So now we call the proud blessed, for those who do wickedness are raised up; they even tempt God and go free.'" ¹⁶ Then those who feared the LORD spoke to one another, and the LORD listened and heard them; so a **book of remembrance was written before Him for those who fear the LORD and who meditate on His name.** ¹⁷ "They shall be Mine," says the LORD of hosts, "On the day that I make them My jewels. And I will spare them as a man spares his own son who serves him." ¹⁸ Then you shall again discern between the righteous and the wicked, between one who serves God and one who does not serve Him.

In Verse 7, Where God tells them, "Return to me, and I will return to you", their response is., "In what way shall we return?" The reason they ask this is because their mentality was "We never left"! But this scripture tells us that when you hold back your tithe AND offering, you are spiritually walking away from Him!! That's a big deal! And this is NEVER preached, but it's scriptural. In Fact, Paul teaches us that giving is a sign of maturing faith.

Romans 12:3-8 NKJV

³ For I say, through the grace given to me, to everyone who is among you, not to think *of himself* more highly than he ought to think, but to think soberly, as **God has dealt to each one a measure of faith.** ⁴ For as we have many members in one body, but all the members do not have the same function, ⁵ so we, *being* many, are one body in Christ, and individually members of one another. ⁶ Having then gifts differing according to the grace that is given to us, *let us use them:* if prophecy, *let us prophesy* in proportion to our faith; ⁷ or ministry, *let us use it* in *our* ministering; he who teaches, in teaching; ⁸ he who exhorts, in exhortation; **he who gives, with liberality;** he who leads, with diligence; he who shows mercy, with cheerfulness.

Hebrews 13:17: _____

_____

_____

_____

_____

Obedience is good, but honor is required for blessing. Many of you have been taught out of Malachi as a mandate, and a rule, looking like it's a switch we flip by obedience, and we know obedience IS BETTER than sacrifice. But it's elementary. The blessing of honor is doing what you do because you love the one you do it for, not because you're told to.

Matthew 6:31-34
"So don't worry about these things, saying, 'What will we eat? What will we drink? What will we wear?' 32 These things dominate the thoughts of unbelievers, but your heavenly Father already knows all your needs. 33 Seek the Kingdom of God above all else, and live righteously, and he will give you everything you need. 34 "So don't worry about tomorrow, for tomorrow will bring its own worries. Today's trouble is enough for today.

Tithing is a response of obedience, giving is a response of trust, and walking in blessing.

Matthew 6:24: _____
_____
_____
_____
_____

Tithing:

In 1 Chronicles 29:1-20 David gives tremendously, and calls Israel to give. Read it.

Scholars have estimated that they gave in approximation, 190 tons of gold, 375 tons of silver, 675 tons of bronze, & 3750 tons of iron!

Leviticus 27:30-31:

_____

_____

_____

_____

_____

A better understanding of how that applies today, is that if you miss an opportunity to give tithe, and keep it, that you not only pay it back next time, but add 20%!!

The word "tithe" – means tenth

God commanded Israel to give a tithe of everything. Everything. Their produce, their land, their belongings, everything. The yearly tithe went taken for three different reasons: For the priests (Numbers 18:21-24). This was because the Levites received no inheritance of land, so they had to be provided for by the people. Secondly, it went to provide for community celebrations (see Deuteronomy 12:17-18 & Deuteronomy 14:22-23). And also, every third year they gave a tithe to help poor and needy (Deuteronomy 14:28-29, Deuteronomy 26:12-13). This went to taking care of the orphans and widows, the needy, etc.

Those three categories of tithing were not the same, but three different tithes. IT wasn't a tenth split three ways. It was a tenth required three times. The first tenth for the priests required once a year, the second given once a year, and the third, once every three years. The Israelites were required by God to give 23% of their income every year. The bare minimum that the Bible required for Israel to represent their covenant with God was 23% of their yearly income.

God instituted a way for them to give in accordance to what they had, out of everything they owned. And in our scripture, the millions of tons given to the temple were on top of their 23%!! That is walking in blessing!

According to Daveramsey.com – December 2008 statistics:
""*Americans who earn less than $10,000 gave 2.3 percent of their income to religious organizations, whereas those who earn $70,000 or more gave only 1.2 percent." While the actual percentages are slightly higher for Christians who regularly attend church, the pattern is similar. Households of committed Christians making less than $12,500 per year give away roughly 7 percent of their income, a figure no other income bracket beats until incomes rise above $90,000 (they give away 8.8 percent).*

"If members of historically Christian churches in the United States had raised their giving to the Old Testament's minimum standard of giving (10% of income) in 2000, an additional $139,000,000,000 a year would become available assist in Christian based mission work."

Giving:

    Giving is a command from Jesus, it is not optional.
Matthew 6:1-2 NLT

    [2] <u>When you give</u> to someone in need…..

God's plan is not that you have a poverty spirit. A poverty spirit always feels like their resources are limited. God never intended for us to live in poverty in any area of our lives. But he does want us to be good stewards over what he has given us, so he won't be wasting good seed on us because we're not responsible.

David said, "I have been young, and now I am old, and I have never seen the righteous forsaken, or his descendants begging for bread." (Psalm 37:25)

"The doorway to breaking the spirit of poverty is giving" – Karen Wheaton

Genesis 13:2: _____

_____

_____

I have full blown arguments with myself sometimes. When I'm driving down the road, and get hungry and want something. First I rationalize that I can spend $4.55 at McDonalds on two snack wraps, grilled and an unsweet tea. But then I start arguing that I should have packed a lunch, and don't need to spend the money just because you didn't take time to make your lunch.

What we love about tithing is that it is specific and proportionate to our income; we know how much we "have" to give. Which, ironically, is the same thing we hate about giving. That it is NOT proportionate to our income, it is out of our heart's overflow, and our good stewardship that we are permitted to give more, and more. And that scares us because we love our money going to us...

Giving was a biblical command that was not specified or limited by amount, size, value, quality or purpose.

Giving was done to show honor to people:

2 Samuel 8:2: _____
_____
_____

Daniel 2:48: _____
_____
_____
_____

Giving was done as a means of celebration:

Revelation 11:10:

_____

_____

_____

_____

Amy Carmichael once said, "It is possible to give without loving, but it is impossible to truly love, without giving."

Damon Thompson – "If you've been saved more than a year, and all you give is your tithe, you are in sin."

We are never more like God than when we give.

Mark 12:41-44 NLT
⁴¹ Jesus sat down near the collection box in the Temple and watched as the crowds dropped in their money. Many rich people put in large amounts. ⁴² Then a poor widow came and dropped in two small coins. ⁴³ Jesus called his disciples to him and said, "I tell you the truth, this poor widow has given more than all the others who are making contributions. ⁴⁴ For they gave a tiny part of their surplus, but she, poor as she is, has given everything she had to live on."

A man is not measured by what he has, but by what has him. Some people own houses, and some people, their houses own them. There is a difference between being rich and being wealthy. Wealthy people refuse to be reduced by their balance sheet and their wealth never has them. Rich people's self-esteem is attached directly to their "profit and loss" statement. But princes do not work for money, they work for the King. Slaves work for money.

The older brother of the prodigal was out working in the field when his brother returned, yet he was their heir to inherit all of his father's possessions, but he worked, nonetheless.

2 Corinthians 9:6-12 NKJV
 6 But this *I say:* He who **sows sparingly will also reap sparingly,** and he who sows **bountifully will also reap bountifully.** 7 *So let* each one **give as he purposes in his heart, not grudgingly or of necessity;** for God loves a cheerful giver. 8 And God *is* able to make **all grace** abound toward you, that you, always having all sufficiency in all *things,* may have an abundance for every good work. 9 As it is written: "He has dispersed abroad, He has given to the poor; His righteousness endures forever." 10 Now may He who supplies seed to the sower, and bread for food, supply and multiply the seed you have *sown* and increase the fruits of your righteousness, 11 while *you are* enriched in everything

for all liberality, which causes thanksgiving through us to God. ¹² For the administration of this service not only supplies the needs of the saints, but also is abounding through many thanksgivings to God,

Verse 7 - Not out of necessity – do not give out of it being required.... Not out of obedience to the call, but from the heart.

I have three challenges I want to submit to you to strive to achieve, and there is no time limit. These goals are lifelong; they are character goals that do not end.

1 – give an offering EVERY TIME I'm asked.

If you have to postdate a check because McDonalds won the fight all week, you give EVERY TIME. Because here's the deal, if we just gave our tithe regularly, the church would rarely have to ask you to give to cover a need.

2 – Consider my stewardship so that I will have more to give to the Kingdom. I have set myself to get my finances in order to the point where I can one day give 50% of my income. Why? Because I want to have the foundation of this church built so that God can release his blessing over it.

3 – I will start looking for needs in my community and if I can, I will meet the need myself. Do things for people just because you can!

Today, as you close out this devotion, take a few moments and pray and write down some commitments to becoming a giver. And come back later and journal how God has blessed you!

_____

_____

_____

_____

_____

_____

_____

_____

_____

_____

_____

_____

_____

_____

Chapter 4

"Kingdom Community"

How God designed His Church

If our position is "In Christ", then the fruit produced out of that position is that old things are passed away; all things are in fact, new! So, if old things have not passed away, we must recognize, admit and do whatever adjustments that needs to be made to get back "in Christ".

False Christianity is simply anything we label as Christianity that does not come in the nature of Christ. So, WWJD is not just a wrist band, but a serious consideration.

Today's lesson is about **your commitment to His Kingdom and to the making of this community of believers.**

Half surrender, halfway commitment, halfway dedication is not commitment at all.

When Jesus came, He died and rose again, and in doing so, He did NOT do away with the law, but replaced it with a greater law….

Romans 8:2-5 NKJV

² For the <u>law of the Spirit of life</u> in Christ Jesus has made me free from <u>the law of sin and death</u>. ³ For what the law could not do in that it was weak through the flesh, God *did* by sending His own Son in the likeness of sinful flesh, on account of sin: He condemned sin in the flesh, ⁴ that the righteous requirement of the law might be fulfilled in us who do not walk according to the flesh but according to the Spirit. ⁵ For those who live according to the flesh set their minds on the things of the flesh, but those *who live* according to the Spirit, the things of the Spirit.

So, the law of flesh (sin and death) is replaced with a law of the Spirit of Life, which is found IN Christ. And when God gives us a standard, or a model, it is our level of commitment that causes us to follow through with our word concerning that law.

Passion is not relegated to age, gender, denomination, or location. Your Passion is solely relegated to target worth. The reason why most people can't follow him and blind men can (Matthew 9:27) is because they see him as worthy and the others don't!

Jonathan Edwards - "God's purpose for my life was that I have a passion for God's glory and that I have a passion for my joy in that glory, and that these two are one passion. If the heart be chiefly and directly fixed on God, and the soul engaged to glorify him, some degree of religious affection will be the effect and attendant of it."

Your responsibility is not to look pretty when you get to church. Your responsibility is that everyone that walks in this door experiences a real fire with the **real Jesus**. God is not after your attendance to a house of worship on Sundays. The Bible was not written by people who attended church just on Sundays. And it was not written to people who only attended church on Sunday mornings!

This is not about joining a Church. It's about becoming a Real Christian, in a real community. Because in a community, we're not jealous of each other's giftings. In a community, we're ok that you go worship with other believers. In a community, relationships take top priority. Relationships with God; relationships with each other!

Community is the gate to dominion! We know how to have church, but we do not know how to change culture? For most the answer is no, and it's because we are operating in a communion that facilitates church growth and not operating in a communion that facilitates dominion. We've exchanged popularity for dominion, and we'd rather be celebrated than influential.

Community is a compound word from two words = "common unity". The beauty of being a part of community is that your inability to do things well does not disqualify you. Only your unwillingness to commit disqualifies you.

Satan fears community because it opens the door to dominion.

Acts 2:42-47 (NLT)

^{42} All the believers devoted themselves to the apostles' teaching, and to fellowship, and to sharing in meals (including the Lord's Supper), and to prayer. ^{43} A deep sense of awe came over them all, and the apostles performed many miraculous signs and wonders. ^{44} And all the believers met together in one place and shared everything they had. ^{45} They sold their property and possessions and shared the money with those in need. ^{46} They worshiped together at the Temple each day, met in homes for the Lord's Supper, and shared their meals with great joy and generosity—^{47} all the while praising God and enjoying the goodwill of all the people. And each day the Lord added to their fellowship those who were being saved.

<u>Let's look at what makes Community and then commit to making it happen:</u>

1.) <u>**They all believed**</u>

We have to start living this thing like we really believe it. Believing is something changes the way you treat it.

How do you define salvation?

_____

_____

_____

_____

Romans 10:9 (look it up, write it down)

_____

_____

_____

_____

So, the definition of salvation is confession of Christ, and believing in your heart. If you TRULY believe in the change that takes place in your heart, that change is forced into your lifestyle. If there's not a change, then what you did was not getting saved. You may have repeated a prayer, but you are not a believer, and you are not saved. We have to start believing again in the power of God!

Do you believe in the power of the Holy Spirit? _____

Does your life show that? ____

Do you believe that God has the power to restore? _____ Do you live like that? _____

Do you believe that when you pray that God will heal, set free, deliver, save, restore, protect, guide, give wisdom, or do you just hope??? We have to get out of the rituals of prayer, and believe. The first church believed to the point that they didn't have to pray to heal people. Do you understand what that just said?! That when there was a need, they didn't pray for it, they commanded it to be whole!!! Because they already lived in prayer!!! They're prayer life was so community driven, that all they did was speak, and Heaven invaded earth. Because they so believed.

2.) All the Believers committed themselves

The KJV version says "Steadfastly" – which means "continual care". There was a constant knowing in them to be a part of this "bigger thing". They made up their minds that they were going to do this thing, regardless of the cost. They didn't know how to do it, they just decided that they were going to do it, and in community, they became a force that no nation could stop! We must re-define devotion from the thought that it is just a 3 minute word from Oswald Chambers in the morning that we, for the most part, cannot relate to our life.

The big question is, "have you done this?"
_____

Have you cared enough about your church to be Committed? _____

To be steadfast? _____

3.) <u>They were committed to the Apostle's teachings</u>

They were not concerned with opinions. They were not concerned with traditions. They were <u>continually caring</u> for the revelation word that they were receiving from their Apostles. This is not about reading your Bible. This is about devotion to the point that it pours out of you constantly.

This is memorizing the Word.
Do you do this? _____

This is preaching the Word.
Do you do this? _____

This is becoming an embodiment of the Word.
Do you do this? _____

They were hungry to know more from God.
Are you? _____

They were hungry to hear from their Apostles.
Are you? _____

They were giving continual care for the word...
Are you? _____

In the Book, Radical, by David Platt (You should read it), an excerpt tells us:
"Imagine being in Sudan. You walk into a thatched hut with a small group of Sudanese church leaders, and you sit down to teach them God's Word. As soon as you start, you lose eye contact with all of them. No one is looking at you, and you hardly see their eyes the rest of the time. The reason is because they're writing down every word you say. They come up to you afterward and say, 'Teacher, we are going to take everything we have learned from God's Word, translate it into our languages, and teach it in our tribes.' They were not listening to receive but to reproduce."

He goes on to ask the self-examining question, "How can I listen to his Word so that I am equipped to teach this Word to others?"

Note taking is a mark of your commitment.
Do you take notes when someone is speaking? _____

Are you devoted to the teachings of God? ____

IF yes, then ask yourself, where's the fruit? Where are your notebooks full of learned things, and how are you applying them so that you can teach them to others? This is not meant to make you feel bad; it is giving you permission to do more than attend church. Because if you're not doing these things, then you are not a part of community, according to the Biblical definition of community. This is the standard that they set for us!

4.) <u>They were committed to fellowship</u>

They just like being around each other. And it was a pure love for each other that fueled it. There were no competitions to be liked, or accepted, or used in ministry. In community, everyone wants everyone else to succeed and do well, and we genuinely enjoy talking to each other and hanging out. Not only did they have devotion for learning, but they were also devoted to each other's company. No one had to organize events to make them come together… But a common love for God with a common love for His word drew them to each other. And they stayed devoted to it…

Regardless of feelings, they knew fellowship was vital to growing in Kingdom!

Do you love being with the people of this church?
_____

Do you only attend "Church" services, or are you longing for daily interaction?
_____

This is what makes us a community of believers

5.) **They were devoted to sharing to meet the needs of others**

They were devoted in sharing in meals...

Think about it this way, the only real needs that they had were food and shelter. They needed to eat, and they needed a place to escape the weather, and sleep. That's it, and each one gave to help facilitate that.... Satan has tied our hands in this area by convincing us that we make our money for our pleasure. And the American way is to get into debt, and live paycheck to paycheck and give God excuses why we can't help...

Look at how you spend your finances...

Where does your majority of your money go?
_____

What percent do you give to help others?
_____

Matthew 25:31-46 – read it!!!

You're not rich or even well off, until you have no need, AND, the people around you have no need....

Do you, with a true heart of compassion, give of yourself to meet the needs? _____

If not, you're not community!!!

6.) <u>They were devoted to prayer</u>

The greatest force on Earth that we have is our ability to communicate with our Father in Heaven, and such a powerful tool is considered by most to be the most dreaded, boring time that we rarely want to take time to involve in our lives. If you've been saved for more than six months and you do not have a consistent, growing, burning, fiery prayer life, then you should re-evaluate whether or not you're really saved...

Several years ago, statistics in a mainline denomination showed that the "American Christian" spends about 4 minutes a <u>week</u> average in prayer. And the "American Evangelical Pastor" spends an average of 17 minutes a week in prayer. There is no way we can call ourselves Christ-like living like that...

Think about it, every teenager at every school claims to be "saved". Everyone you work with claim to go to church! But do they bear fruit…?

Why, in your opinion, is prayer so hard?
_____
_____
_____
_____
_____

Maybe it's hard because we do not see or feel the immediate results from it, but if we want to see them get out of wheelchairs, we must be people devoted to community, and community is bathed in prayer.

The more you pray, the more you'll see how inadequate your prayer life is, and want to do it more. People who don't pray will NEVER walk in Kingdom power, and will ALWAYS struggle with the lust of the flesh. Because they are living for self.

For every seed sown, there is fruit that is born from it… If you plant apple seeds, eventually you get _____ (gave you an easy one)

So, the consequences, or fruit, of these efforts are shown in the rest of the scripture:

Read Acts 2:42-47 slowly (highlight what you like)

The Consequences of Community:

7.) A sense of awe – amazement
Read verse 43 again

They were just in awe at what God was doing! Because they cultivated community correctly, they were able to see and perform many signs and wonders!!!!

The Fruit of unity is Holy Spirit dominion, and fruit of Holy Spirit is displayed through gifts...

8.) They wanted to be around each other often
Read Verse 44 again

Their day did not consist of what they *had to do*; their days consisted of what they were going to **get to do** with each other... And it wasn't forced thinking, it was a natural byproduct (fruit) of the effort sown...

9.) Shared everything
Verse 44 again

In community, it's for the common good. They understood this!! I don't mind you having what I have because I know your heart is pure...

IS that your mindset? _____ If not, maybe you need to get inside of community!!

10.) <u>Sold property for provision</u>

Whatever it costs me!! They were willing to give up something of value of their own, in order to meet the needs of those around them, with no strings attached

11.) <u>Worshipped together daily in the Temple</u>

This is Beautiful!!! They met in homes DAILY, not once on Sunday for an hour!!! They shared meals with joy and generosity!!!! This is the formula for Holy Spirit dominion... **This is the only way that it works...** This is what is required of us as believers to carry a new mantle!

The question is, ARE YOU WILLING?

This is it!!! This is where you have to decide if you're going to really commit, or if you're going to go back to your old life!?!?

I want you to take some time and write down what this devotion has sparked in you to do and what you are committing to, and what you want to see happen in our community.

_____

_____

Chapter 5

"The power of Spiritual Authority"

You weren't meant to be a Lone Ranger

Read Psalm 91:1-2 (write it down): _____

_____

_____

_____

_____

_____

_____

Where will you abide? _____

In this lesson on commitment, we are going to focus on what it means to be obediently "under" God's authority.

I. The concept of being "Under Cover".

When you hear the concept of being undercover, what do you think of?

_____
_____
_____
_____
_____
_____

The term "Undercover" is simply the safety found in your hidden identity. Someone that is operating undercover can move freely about WITHOUT being apprehended by the enemy. The definition for the word undercover always has PROTECTION and FREEDOM in it.

How does undercover apply to Christians?_____
_____
_____
_____
_____

Stop. Go back and re-read Psalm 91:1-2.

This passage is the simplest version of how being undercover applies to Christians. The Biblical definition of the word shows that the one who is under cover, is the one who is under God's AUTHORITY.

While in the garden, Adam and Eve enjoyed the freedom and protection that come from being under God's cover.

Look up Genesis 3:7 and WRITE it down:

_____
_____
_____
_____
_____

The moment that they voluntarily disobeyed the word of God, they found themselves desperately searching for the thing that they had given up. They were in need to "cover themselves."

Their disobedience to God and his authority, robbed ALL of mankind from the protection and freedom that was once known.

What does it mean to have AUTHORITY over something?

_____
_____
_____
_____
_____
_____

Authority in its basic form is defined as something that has the right to command or control something or someone. This means, that the things that influence your decisions have garnered authority in your life. (I.E. sports, fashion, boyfriend, girlfriend.)

What have you given authority to? (Be honest)

1._____

2._____

3._____

4._____

5._____

I bet like most of us, you have given authority to these things in your life without even realizing that you are doing it.

Authority is not a very popular word in today's modern American church. This is mainly because people simply have too much PRIDE. Yet, by rejecting proper authority, we lose sight of the great benefits and protection that come along with it.

ONLY someone that is operating from the position of AUTHORITY can AUTHORIZE someone to be under cover.

II. Confronting Rebellion.

"I'm just not going to submit to Authority, unless I first agree with it." How many times have you heard this phrase said in today's church? Better yet, how many times have YOU said this????

What are some excuses that you give, when you reject Authority, BE HONEST WITH YOURSELF?

1._____

2._____

3._____

Consider all that rebellion does:

    1. Caused Lucifer to fall

    2. Caused Adam to fall

    3. Causes Man to fall

Most rebellion is not blatant but subtle.

To consider what rebellion is, you must first understand the type of Authority or Government in which Christianity is operated under. America is operated under a DEMOCRATIC government. Christianity is operated under a KINGDOM mindset.

What do you think is the difference between the two types of governments?

_____

_____

_____

_____

A kingdom has rank, order, and authority. That gifts, blessings, anointing, and favor are all passed through connection. In other words, as long as you stay in the house of the King, then you get to inherit everything that the King has.

In a democracy, everyone gets a vote, so leaders must appeal to the people in order to keep their position. A democratic approach WILL NOT bring the very freedom that we seek. In a democracy, we have to please people to get their vote.

In a Kingdom, you only have to please the King.

Now that you understand more about the AUTHORITY, on which you are to operate under, you can understand how to properly obey it.

"There is freedom in submission and bondage in rebellion."

It is NOT possible to submit to God's Authority, but not submit to his delegated authority.

Romans 13:1-2 WRITE IT DOWN!!!!!

_____
_____
_____
_____
_____
_____
_____

ALL AUTHORITY ORIGINATES FROM HIM!!!!!!

To go against Authority that GOD has ordained to be in your life is REBELLION.

Hebrews 13:17 KJV
 17 Obey them that have the rule over you, and submit yourselves: for they watch for your souls, as they that must give account, that they may do it with **JOY**, and not with **GRIEF**: for that is unprofitable for **YOU**.

This is more than just you being obedient:

Honoring and submitting to authority and obedience to authority look identical on the outside. Just like holiness and legalism look the same on the outside. Two different people can serve by cleaning the church and one is doing it because it was asked of them. The other is because they honor the authority over them. What they do may look the same, but in time, the fruit of the blessing of a right heart approach will begin to show in one life, while the other will do like most of us do, and get frustrated that we are not seeing results when we are "doing what we're supposed to do".

Simple obedience is only done out of respect for authority and their position. You do what you're told at your job because if you don't the person who told you to do it has the power to remove you from that job.

The blessing of being "under cover" is produced through you believing in the person leading you to the point where even if you do not have faith in their decisions, even if you do not have understanding in why they chose to lead the way they do, even in spite of that, you submit... You don't bring dishonor to the leader that God put you under.

Your "need to understand why" is not an excuse to bring dishonor to the institution of His church and worse, it's not an excuse to continue to see your life be unfruitful, and you continue to live under that curse.

III. Division and Disobedience

Division is made up of the words:

_____ and _____.

(You should have put "Di" and "vision")

"Di" means 2

The simple understanding is that the word division means "two visions".

So, what does the Bible say about division?

2 Corinthians 1:10-13 (write it down)

_____
_____
_____
_____
_____
_____
_____
_____
_____

Luke 11:17 (write it down)

_____
_____
_____
_____

1 Corinthians 12:21-26 (Write it down)

_____
_____
_____
_____

_____
_____
_____
_____
_____
_____
_____
_____
_____
_____
_____

The Bible clearly states that a Kingdom that is operating under the spirit of division has a lack for power. For a Kingdom divided among itself surely will not prosper.

What does it mean to disobey someone?

_____
_____
_____
_____
_____

To disobey God is to simply go against his Word or the Law that he created.

1 John 3:4 (write it down):

_____

_____
_____
_____
_____
_____
_____

So all "Sin" is simply being governed (given law), and then rejecting or breaking that law. So, to disobey = To Sin. The problem with the church today is that when the word SIN is mentioned, the only thing that comes to mind is the "Gross/Big Sins."

1. Lying - (Ephesians 4:24-25)

2. Drunk - (Ephesians 5:18)

3. Adultery - (1 Corinthians 6:18)

4. Stealing - (Ephesians 4:28)

5. Murder - (1 John 3:15)

But, read the following passage and write it down.

Romans 5:19

_____
_____
_____
_____

_____

Adam did not "Gamble or Murder or Steal" in the Garden, he simply did not submit and obey the Word of God.

Not ALL sin is "Gross," but all sin DESTROYS.

Romans 6:23 (write it down):

_____
_____
_____
_____
_____

SIMPLE DISOBEDIENCE IS SIN!!!!

Read Matthew 22:1-14 The Parable of the Wedding Supper.

Seriously, read it…

None of the reasons that were given as to why they couldn't attend the wedding would be viewed as illegitimate reasons; they simply did not obey the King. With a better understanding of what sin is, the widespread deception and disobedience of God's Word can be STOPPED!!!!

IV. Disobedience in Us as a Church

In Matthew 24:12-13, it is clearly pointed out that sin will run rampant through the Church. It was written about the believers, not the sinners. If you were to ask many typical Sunday morning Congregations the two following questions, I am sure that you could predict their answers?

1. Is the world full of sin? The answer would be a resounding YES

2. Is the church full of sin? The answer would be a firm NO

If this is true, then why does the Book of Matthew clearly state that SIN will run rampant everywhere, and the love of many will grow cold?

This is due to the DECEPTION of the state of the church that is present.

What is the root cause of the deception of the church?

James 1:22 (write it down)

_____
_____
_____

The cause of the deception of the church is simply DISOBEDIENCE.

Many people would ask, how could the deception run rampant in the church, and that can be found in 3 different areas of the Bible. (WRITE THEM DOWN)

2 Thessalonians 2:10

_____
_____
_____
_____
_____

Ezekiel 33: 30-31

_____
_____

_____
_____
_____
_____

2 Timothy 3:1-4

_____
_____
_____
_____
_____
_____
_____
_____

The two keys to stop the deception from running rampant through the church are:

    1. Hear and OBEY the Word of God.

    2. We must LOVE truth more than anyone or anything else.

V. The Secret Power of "LAWLESSNESS"

2 Thessalonians 2:7

_____
_____
_____
_____

_____

The mystery or secret of the Lawlessness in the church is simply that, it's a mystery and a secret. That is because with believers, lawlessness would not be effective if blatant, but only if subtle and deceptive. Satan is the master of deception. (John 8:44)

Consider the following scenario: Satan was able to lead a third of the angels in the uprising against God. (Revelation 12:3-4) This deception took place in a perfect environment, in the very presence of GOD. He was able to deceive Eve, who lived in a perfect environment, free from influence and demonic rule. What makes you think it will be difficult for him to mislead multitudes in the earthly environment????? Satan was able to deceive Eve through her ignorance.

IGNORANCE IS A BREEDING GROUND FOR DECEPTION!!

There are 2 different ways to receive knowledge.

1. Communicated Knowledge - Which means that you hear it from someone who heard if from someone else. Second hand knowledge.

2. Revealed Knowledge - You hear it for yourself.

The best way to receive knowledge is REVEALED KNOWLEDGE. The problem with Communicated Knowledge is something can be lost in the translation.

Consider the two following passages:

Genesis 2:16-17 (read it)

Genesis 3:1-3 (read it)

Notice any key differences in them?_____
_____
_____
_____
_____

Who did Eve get her information from?

_____

God NEVER said anything about touching it. But when Adam repeated to Eve what God said, something was misinterpreted. This is an example of what can happen when you have heard from another person what God has said, rather than to hear it yourself. Hearing something secondhand makes us more vulnerable to deception.

We all remember the "telephone game" that we played while in Elementary school. By the time the secret was whispered around the whole circle of students, the final thought was TOTALLY DIFFERENT than what was originally started.

1 Timothy 6:10 (Write it down)

_____
_____
_____
_____

_____

This completely disputes the saying that "Money is the root of all evil!" That is not what God said in his Word. This shows that if the only way that you receive information is through Communication (secondhand), that even if one word is misspoken or mistaken, sin can occur. Especially considering the fact, THAT MONEY HELPS TO ADVANCE THE KINGDOM!!!!

You might be wondering, how do I receive revelation knowledge, and not have to rely on others (I.E. pastor, parents, etc...) through communicative knowledge.

The Bible gives at least 3 verses on how to receive this:

Isaiah 66:2: _____
_____
_____

Psalm 25:14: _____
_____
_____
_____

Ecclesiastes 12:13: _____
_____
_____
_____

VI. The Secret of Satan

The strategy of the Satan is as follows:

(We are going to focus on the story of Adam & Eve)

    1. Distort the emphasis of God's command. He makes us question God's motive.

Where does Satan do this to Eve at?_____
_____
_____
_____

    2. Ignores God's generosity and point to His exception. Imply something good was being withheld.

Where is this done at?_____
_____
_____
_____

    3. Seizes the opportunity to undermine God's authority, truthfulness, and integrity.

What verse shows this? _____

Once the character of God and his integrity are brought into question, there no longer remains any reason for submission to His Authority in any matter. With disobedience, becomes spiritual death. Flesh now becomes the strong taskmaster and has Authority in their lives.

SATAN'S TACTIC OF OPERATION THEN, DIFFERS LITTLE TODAY.

James 1:16-17

_____
_____
_____
_____
_____

That is Bible and the writer of it makes sure that as believers, we should not fall to the same secret power of the lawlessness that enticed Eve. Partial obedience is not obedience in the eyes of God. Rather, it is rebellion.

Now that we know how Satan deceives, let's take a look at how God restores disobedience.

VII. Restoration

The first thing that God does is that He attempts to reach a person through conviction. Two things happen during this phase:

    1. We as a people feel the conviction on our heart, and change or ways, or

    2. We begin to justify our disobedience.

Justification does 2 things:

a. We become positioned to repeat the act

b. Conviction becomes less and less. Reasoning takes its place

Deception hides the truth and our conscience is seared.

When is a time that you felt convicted about something, but continued to do it anyways?

_____

_____

_____

_____

2. God sends a prophetic messenger

   The prophet comes so that the people have their eyes open to see the true ways of God. (Samuel to Saul)

3. God attempts to reach us through Judgment.

   Psalm 119:67

   _____

   _____

   1 Corinthians 11:30-31

   _____

   _____

   _____

   _____

VII. The Christian "MAN"

A.W. Tozer says the following about obedience:

"The man that believes will obey; failure to obey is convincing proof that there is no true faith present. To attempt the impossible God must give faith or there will be none, and He gives faith to the obedient heart only."

The Bible states that when everyone begins to obey, and focus on one singular vision, the Kingdom will display TRUE POWER.

VIII. Visual Reminder

MAKE IT A PURPOSE TO ALLIGN YOURSELF WITH NOT ONLY THE VISION OF THE CHURCH, BUT ALSO TO THE WORD OF GOD. DO NOT FORGET THAT WE ARE CALLED TO BE A CHURCH AND PEOPLE OF POWER. THE ONLY WAY THAT THIS CAN BE DONE IS THROUGH TRUE OBEDIENCE.

WRITE DOWN ONE OF THE BIBLE VERSES FROM THIS LESSON ON A SHEET OF PAPER AND TAPE IT ON YOUR MIRROR OR DOOR. MAKE YOURSELF A REMINDER OF THE AUTHORITY THAT YOU WILL WALK IN, WHEN YOU SUBMIT YOURSELF TO HIS AUTHORITY.

PRAY FOR TRUE DIRECTION AND SPIRITUAL AUTHORITY....

DO IT TODAY!!! RIGHT NOW!!!! WITHOUT YOUR TRUE SUMBISSION TO THE KING, THIS WHOLE CHURCH SUFFERS... YOU ARE PIVOTAL TO THIS!!!!!

Write down any revelations or commitments you are making today concerning today's lesson

_____

_____

_____

_____

_____

_____

_____

_____

_____

_____

_____

_____

Chapter 6

"Why Christians Quit"

Recognizing patterns that will pull you away and removing them

Turn to Psalm 78

One of the greatest frustrations of all spiritual leaders is that whatever the investment we make in people, we have to watch almost helplessly as those people take the great potential of the experience and put it back into the wretchedly idol filled life outside of church. Every wondered why the youth camp high never lasts? Because the effort you made during youth camp, or during this week is not maintained once you get your phone back, once you get your boyfriend/girlfriend back, and once you start watching the stupid television again.

We strip away all idols and distractions during times like this and then have to send you home where you will not have us motivating you to do it on your own.

It's been said that good seed (the word) planted

in good ground (your soul) will bear good fruit. But that's not true. Good seed has the potential to bear good food when planted in good ground, but what they don't tell you is that the ground is not the only factor. You can have the best soil in America, but it be located in somewhere like Iowa. You can have the choicest of orange seeds, but oranges will NEVER grow in Iowa. Even though the soil is good, and the seed is good, the environment is not good.

All that you accomplish in your own personal devotional life will be for nothing if you are not willing to change the environment you live in. The fact is that oranges can actually grow in Iowa... If someone builds a massively large hot house. If someone invests greatly into changing the environment. That's what you have to do.

We are going to move from prayer into application, so take great time and effort into applying what this lesson is teaching you so that you will be willing to make effort to not let this die.

Most American Christians live far short of the true Biblical standard of devotion. It's very rare to find someone who has lived a consistent growing life since their conversion.

We even find in Scripture, that there are people who lose their fire:

Please list in your own words how these Bible people actually lost their passion and fire:

- David: _____
  _____

- Peter: _____
  _____

- The Prodigal son: _____
  _____

What about people like:

- Judas: _____
  _____

- Demas: _____
  _____

(Look them up if you are not sure about them)

_____
_____

Psalm 78:1-11 read it!

This Psalm gives us great insight into how not to quit, and why most do

1. **People lose their fire because they are not properly taught**

⁵ For He established a testimony in Jacob, and appointed a law in Israel, which He commanded our fathers, that they should make them known to their children;

Your faith must be built by fathers giving instruction…

Quickly think of some things you were taught from a spiritual father in your life:

_____

_____

_____

_____

_____

Most people don't understand real Christianity, and will never live consistently, simply because most pastors don't understand their role.

Ephesians 4:11-15 (read it)

The role of the pastor, Apostle, and other gifts listed is not just to preach to you. They are responsible to grow you. Does your pastor, Apostle, teacher, invest in your life outside of standing behind a pulpit? ____

If the answer is no, then you need to make yourself available to their personal investment. If you ask him/her to do more than just preach to you and they are not willing to, then you should seriously find someone of spiritual authority that will teach and invest in you. Too many people are stuck in the tradition of attending a place of worship and not being challenged to grow, but since grandma started that church, we are going to be faithful here.

The definition of faithful is not, "Doing nothing for a long time." That's not faithful... That's torture. You are to be taught so that you are growing.

Let's take a small quiz to see just how "taught" you are...

What is the significance of the Sermon on the Mount?

_____
_____.

Why did Jesus wash the disciple's feet?

_____
_____
_____

What is the purpose of Paul's letters?

_____
_____
_____.

What are the gifts of the Spirit for?

_____
_____
_____

Why do we even have the Old Testament?

_____
_____

We lose most of our battles because we are ill equipped.

Do you memorize scripture? _____ The Bible tells us to hide the word of God in our hearts that we would not sin against God. People who struggle with sin, really struggle with the word. Do you conquer the sinful thoughts tempting you from the Devil, or do you indulge in them? _____ What foundation of teaching do you have that keeps you consistent??

You are not solely responsible for your growth. You do play a part, called application and effort. But there is also responsibility on your spiritual leader to do more than preach to you, but to hold you accountable, and teach you, and push you, and love you.

When men of God fail to testify of God through their words and their lifestyles, they will raise children who will utterly fail at being Godly in their walk.

It's hard enough to walk that way with a man of God giving instruction... Imagine how impossible it is for someone without proper instruction. This is why you thinking that Bible study is boring, and teachings are not as important as "Worship services" on Sundays, you are mistaken. They are just as important!

You want to stay hot, you must cultivate a hot house, and you do that through the pushing into spiritual authority. You do that through consistent church attendance. You do that through your servanthood! You do that through loving and committing to the house of God and always being willing to let Spiritual authority push you.

2. <u>People lose their fire due to their lack a total commitment</u>

Look at the beginning of verse 9 again,

"The children of Ephraim, *being* _____ *and* _____ _____

They were armed and ready to go... but lost their commitment. They had the look of an army; they had the right weapons, they had the armor! They had the look. Just when it came time to fight, turned around and quit. Commitment does more than have the look!

Think about a time, or several times, in your walk with God where you were striving to do what you knew was right, wearing the right clothes, saying the right words, looking the part, and when you found yourself facing a real fight (temptation, compromise, etc.) you ran instead of committing through the pain of the battle: (This can be anything, it's for your eyes only, so be honest with yourself)

_____

_____

_____

_____

_____

_____

When we're faced with real warfare, it shows us the truth of our commitment. And when you're really striving to grow, one threat can put out your fire quickly, and we tend to blame it on the circumstance. "I quit because it was too hard". "I didn't have anyone to hold me accountable". "It wasn't that big of deal at the time"!

But the reality is that it wasn't the fault of the "thing", it's just that when you boil it down to truth, you were just not really committed. And if you're not really committed, you cannot stay on fire.

Galatians 5:7 (Message)

⁷ You were running superbly! Who cut in on you, deflecting you from the true course of obedience? This detour doesn't come from the One who called you into the race in the first place. And please don't toss this off as insignificant.

The Greek word for Devil is *diobolos*

- Dia – means "to penetrate"
- Bolos – means "to throw repeatedly"

Devil is not his name, it's his job description! Devil means, "He throws repeatedly until he breaks through into your mindset" And most of us, who are strong, are strong most of the time, BUT.... If he keeps trying to get you to quit, or distract you, eventually, we all find ourselves not as committed to the cause as we once were.

What is it inside of me that makes me quit when I should be fighting? _____

_____

_____

_____

What is it in me that I will tolerate being defeated to the point where I make an excuse as to why I am not even fighting?

_____

_____

_____

What makes you comfortable living in your defeat when you used to fight? _____

_____

_____

What inside of you makes you okay with the fact that if God asked you to get in the game and pray for someone, you'd have nothing inside of you to pull from? _____

_____

_____

In Ezekiel, there was an army of dry bones that came to life. They had skin, weapons, and were standing at attention, but had no breath in them.

They had the look, but not the commitment to win the fight.

Matthew 24:13 (write it down)

_____

_____

_____

If endurance is the key to winning, we cannot keep settling for false finish lines! We love to talk about what God DID, and never have anything fresh to talk about what God is currently doing. Not because He quit, but because we did... OR... we're content to go with what we knew about Him when we were in a place of pursuit and burning... Reminding ourselves of truths that we no longer even believe! And you, in your own life, can gauge whether you're still burning hot for God, or whether you're sleeping simply by the fact that when attacks come at you, you don't fight.

- When depression hits, what do you do?
- When financial issues rise up, what do you do?
- When temptation comes, how do you respond?

- When sickness comes, and disease is diagnosed?

Does the things that used to disgust you, still disgust you? OR, do the things you used to battle for now seem dull or tolerable to you?

Think about it... What are some things that you tolerate now, (or before this week), that when you were burning for God, you would have never tolerated? Things that would have angered you to see your friends doing, but now you make excuses for doing them yourself (list them, your eyes only):

_____

_____

_____

_____

_____

You cannot hope that your pastor will fight, your leaders will fight, you have to fight. Look at what we tolerate; Look at how we talk, look at what we listen to, look at what we watch, look at how we respond to trials... And ask yourself, "Shouldn't I be fighting harder than I am right now?"

Here's the problem with toleration; when we entertain the Devil instead of warring against him, then we begin to make excuses to justify our behavior; my job, my money, my schedule, my time.

There's an old Chines proverb that says, "An idle mind is the Devil's workshop"

Ecclesiastes 10:18 (write it down):

_____

_____

_____

And the danger with doing nothing when you should be warring is that, by nature, we get bored with doing nothing. And when we get bored, we look for something, anything... Anything that will entertain us when we should be warring. How many times do you get up and go to the fridge when you're not hungry?? You're just bored! How many times do you check your phone to see if anything has changed? If you go out and resolve to dig thirty seven holes with post hole diggers and then fill em back up, I promise you that you will not have time to look for foolish things to do.

If you're not in a dog fight, you're not committed. Commitment is asking you to be faithful even when no one else is! Committing to something goes beyond preparation into demonstration!

Are you committed to prayer even when you don't feel like it? ____

Are you committed to loving people? _____
Are you committed to reaching lost? _____

Are you just wearing the armor, or are you in a fight??? _____

Some people look the look until the arrows start flying and then they are out! This fire will die if you don't commit to living the life of a true Biblical Christian, and you have just wasted a week of your life… Commit!!

3. **<u>People lose their fire because they don't fulfill responsibilities</u>**

Psalm 78:10 (write it down): _____

_____

_____

_____

They don't do ALL that God wants them to do. Notice that it does not tell us that "They forgot".... They just didn't do what they knew to do... Your generation has been excused for not completing anything. And we will quit on God just as easily as we quit on everything and everyone else.

2 Corinthians 8:10-11 (NLT)

[10] Here is my advice: It would be good for you to finish what you started a year ago. Last year you were the first who wanted to give, and you were the first to begin doing it. [11] <u>Now you should finish what you started</u>. Let the eagerness you showed in the beginning be matched now by your giving.

2 Corinthians 10:3-5 (Write it down)

_____

_____

_____

_____

_____

_____

What weapons of warfare??? Obedience – "Bringing into captivity every thought to the <u>obedience</u> of Christ;" The thoughts: way of thinking, coming under submission to obedience.

1 Samuel 15:22-23 (NLT)

²² But Samuel replied, "What is more pleasing to the LORD: your burnt offerings and sacrifices or your obedience to his voice? Listen! Obedience is better than sacrifice, and submission is better than offering the fat of rams. ²³ Rebellion is as sinful as witchcraft, and stubbornness as bad as worshiping idols. So because you have rejected the command of the LORD, he has rejected you as king."

You wanting to do it your way, and have God bless it is disobedience. God puts spiritual authority in your life to make you better. If they are investing in you and asking you to do things that will build you, and keep your fire going and you just chose not to, you are forfeiting your fire for your own preference. Commit to prayer, submission, devotion, servanthood, etc. And watch the fire of God continue to burn in you.

4. People lose their fire because they forget what God has done

Psalm 78:11 (write it down):

_____

_____

_____

"Remember" is the most repeated command in the Bible. To remind ourselves of what God has done, to ensure that we will stay the course. Think of people who are not living the way they should be that once lived for God. They've forgotten the truth of who God was for them. They've forgotten the love of God!

Scriptures:

Then his disciples **remember**ed this prophecy from the Scriptures: "Passion for God's house will consume me." (John 2:17)

After he was raised from the dead, his disciples **remember**ed he had said this, and they believed both the Scriptures and what Jesus had said. (John 2:22)

His disciples didn't understand at the time that this was a fulfillment of prophecy. But after Jesus entered into his glory, they **remember**ed what had happened and realized that these things had been written about him. (John 12:16)

Anyone who doesn't love me will not obey me. And **remember**, my words are not my own. What I am telling you is from the Father who sent me. (John 14:24)

Remember what I told you: I am going away, but I will come back to you again. If you really loved me, you would be happy that I am going to the Father, who is greater than I am. (John 14:28)

"If the world hates you, **remember** that it hated me first." (John 15:18)

Do you **remember** what I told you? 'A slave is not greater than the master.' Since they persecuted me, naturally they will persecute you. And if they had listened to me, they would listen to you. (John 15:20)

Yes, I'm telling you these things now, so that when they happen, you will **remember** my warning. I didn't tell you earlier because I was going to be with you for a while longer. (John 16:4)

Watch out! **Remember** the three years I was with you—my constant watch and care over you night and day, and my many tears for you. (Acts 20:31)

And I have been a constant example of how you can help those in need by working hard. You should **remember** the words of the Lord Jesus: 'It is more blessed to give than to receive.'" (Acts 20:35)

But you are not controlled by your sinful nature. You are controlled by the Spirit if you have the Spirit of God living in you. (And **remember** that those who do not have the Spirit of Christ living in them do not belong to him at all.) (Romans 8:9)

And do you **remember** God's reply? He said, "No, I have 7,000 others who have never bowed down to Baal!" (Romans 11:4)

Yes, but **remember**—those branches were broken off because they didn't believe in Christ, and you are there because you do believe. So don't think highly of yourself, but fear what could happen. (Romans 11:20)

So why do you condemn another believer? Why do you look down on another believer? **Remember**, we will all stand before the judgment seat of God. (Romans 14:10)

Don't tear apart the work of God over what you eat. **Remember**, all foods are acceptable, but it is wrong to eat something if it makes another person stumble. (Romans 14:20)

Remember that Christ came as a servant to the Jews to show that God is true to the promises he made to their ancestors. (Romans 15:8)

You cannot continue this on your own, that's why God designed community. Not church attendance two or three times a week.

Commit today to do your part in keeping your fire going, and our prayer is that you continue to grow so much that when you look back on this week, it will look so elementary to where you are then!!!

Closing commitment: (write down what you commit to based on this teaching): _____

_____

_____

_____

Chapter 7

"Invading this Babylon"

Taking this thing outside of the Church walls

"Any gospel that doesn't work in the marketplace doesn't work!" – Bill Johnson

We have been given authority over this planet. It was first given to us in this commission God gave to mankind in the Garden of Eden (read Genesis 1:28-29). It was forfeited by Adam, but later restored to us by Jesus after His resurrection (read Matthew 28:18). But kingdom authority is different than is typically understood by many believers. It is the authority to set people free from torment and disease, to destroy the works of darkness. It is the authority to move the resources of Heaven through creative expression to meet human need. It is the authority to bring Heaven to earth. It is the authority to serve.

When we, as servants, begin to express the Kingdom of God, it literally rocks this world to its core. Like Jesus, our master, we are both servants and royalty (read Revelation 1:5 and Mark 10:45).

Royalty is my identity. Servanthood is my assignment. Intimacy with God is my life source.

(You should highlight and maybe memorize that statement)

That means that before God, I am intimate. Before people, I am a servant. And before the powers of hell, I'm a ruler with no tolerance for their influence.

There are seven realms of society that must come under the influence of the King and his Kingdom. For that to happen, we, as citizens of the Kingdom, must invade. The dominion of the Lord Jesus is manifest whenever the people of God go forth to serve by bringing the order and blessing of His world into this one. For this invasion to work effectively, we must correct a few misconceptions. In doing so, it is equally important to establish the necessary Kingdom principles in their proper order.

There is no such thing as secular employment for the believer. Once we are born again, everything about us is redeemed for Kingdom purpose. It is all spiritual. Every believer is in full time ministry – only a few have pulpits in sanctuaries. The rest have their pulpits in the world system. Be sure to preach only good news! Understand that an assignment to be in business is as valuable in the Kingdom as is the call to be an evangelist. Embrace your call with faithfulness and thankfulness worthy of the One who called you.

The seven mountains that we are to invade for the Kingdom are as follows:

- Business
- Education
- The Church
- Family
- Arts and entertainment
- Science and medicine
- government

1. **Business**
It's hard to gain favor in a world without prosperity. Prosperity is the primary measure for success in the business arena.

Proverbs 22:29 (Write it down):

_____

_____

_____

But even the world knows that money is not the only measure of true success. Most in business want much more than money for their labors. They want joy, a happy home, life, recognition, and meaningful friendships.

3 John 1:2 (Write it down)

_____

_____

_____

What does John show us to be the true prosperity?

_____

In your opinion, how do we, as Christians invade the business world with the Kingdom?

_____

_____

_____

_____

Tough question, huh!? But it is one that we are called to invade. The kingdom business person has the chance to display a more complete picture of success by focusing on more than money. While there is room for overt ministry in every part of life, it is generally not the outward preaching of the Gospel that secures the place of favor in the eyes of the unbelieving businessperson. It is the divine order a believer has in his or her overall approach to life – to self, family, business, and community.

It is our job to take the church into this world of "Babylonian influence" and bring the kingdom, and we do that by having the attitude of dominion outside of the church. We do that in the business world by working all things with excellence.

Excellence is a Kingdom value, and is not to be confused with perfectionism, which is counterfeit and comes from a religious spirit.

Some of you may be called to be a business owner, or manager. This is just as important as being called to stand behind a pulpit and preach!

2. Education

The Western mindset values reason as the only proper measure of truth, and this actually waters down the gospel of Christ. When we qualify truth based on our own ability to reasonably understand it, then the supernatural then becomes subject to the evaluation of ignorant people.

Invading the educational system is vital to the work of the Kingdom of God. It is educators who shape the mind of tomorrows leaders.

Educators are vital to the Kingdom of God. Our young people need to believe that they will be able to live their entire lives on this earth, and plan accordingly. Get educated, married, have children, all with a Kingdom mindset. Too many generations who experience the outpouring of the Spirit forfeit their desires for training and education in order to do "the Lord's work." As noble as that sounds, it comes from a misunderstanding of real ministry aided by the idea that we will be taken out of here at any moment. The desire to go to Heaven is right and healthy, but it must not replace our commission:

Matthew 6:10 (Write it down):

_____

_____

_____

_____

Read Luke 19:13. What were we commanded to do? _____

We were not commissioned to look into the clouds for His returning. We were commissioned to "occupy" until he comes. How would you define that word "occupy"?: _____

_____

So, given your definition, how do we, as Christians, occupy the earth, until He comes? _____

_____

_____

_____

If the education system is going to improve, it will not be because of the government intervention. It will be because Christians take their calling to educate seriously, and invade this Babylonian system with the true gospel and love of Christ.

Throughout scripture we see that when God's people step up to serve, God backs it up with power. The educational system is begging for our help! This is our time to invade, serve and shine light into a dark world.

Some of you may be called to be a teacher in a school. This is just as important as being called to stand behind a pulpit and preach! We have to invade Babylon!

3. Entertainment

Entertainment meaning the arts, sports, media, etc. Anything we do not invade becomes darker. Matthew 5:14 calls us the "Light of the world". That means that if we are not invading them, they are getting darker, and understand this; invasion is the responsibility of light.

An example of invasion of this mountain is the release of *The Passion of the Christ* in 2004. Christianity invaded Babylon, and thousands of lives were changed because of that movie. In Sports, Tim Tebow, for example, is ridiculed, and mocked, and verbally crucified for kneeling down and thanking God, but His stand in the Babylonian culture has inspired countless young men and women to be outspoken about their faith.

And based on what is being "produced" by Christian companies (i.e. – *Left Behind, Facing the Giants, etc.*), it would seem "sub-par" to the worldly producers. Almost giving the impression that creativity is where we, as Christians, have the biggest challenge in this mountain of influence. The opposite is true! Hollywood has substituted sensuality for creativity! And they have left a huge gap in the area of real originality!

Heaven has what we're looking for! The best novels and plays have yet to be written! The most beautiful songs and melodies are yet to be written. Some of you may be called to invade the entertainment world. This is just as important as being called to stand behind a pulpit and preach! We have to invade Babylon.

4. **The Church**

Mark 8:15 (write it down):

_____

_____

_____

_____

The mentality of the Pharisees places God at the center of everything, but He is worshipped as an impersonal and powerless deity. They excel at traditions that are convenient and reverence that is self-serving. The church has attempted to be relevant by becoming more entertaining to the people. But, as with anything that is geared towards entertainment, you have to improve every week to keep the people happy. This is why Christians have to invade the Church with the true hunger and message of Christ.

What makes the Church a Kingdom entity is not the number of people in attendance, or the sales of CD's or books, even the money to record and put your "show" on television. What makes the Church a Kingdom influence and force of invasion, is when the sole drive behind it is passion, purity, power and people.

Have you ever been to a church, and it felt impersonal? Felt programmed? Felt like you were almost at a presentation, or a play of some sorts, that has a start time and an end time, and we have to get you out in time for the next group to come in for the next presentation?

Did you walk out feeling like you really didn't receive anything of Kingdom importance? _____

We are called to make the Church look like it did in the Book of Acts. Cultural relevance has nothing to do with looking like Acts! If you can pull people out of wheelchairs, you won't need smoke and lights!

Compassion is one of the greatest tools we possess to invade this mountain of influence.

When you walk into church, do you feel personally loved and accepted, or do you feel like cattle being herded in and out?

5. <u>Family</u>

This mountain is slowly being destroyed by Satan at the core of its purpose. The latest statistics show a noticeable drop in the divorce rates in America. However, the reason is not that people are not getting divorced, but rather, that people are not getting married.

The idea of family is all but eroded from the core value system of our country, and that moral decay is slowly settling itself into the church house. We must aggressively pursue the mountain of family. And the way that we invade this mountain is for families to be healthy and not hidden. When relationships are good, and the boundaries of godly disciplines are intact, there is no limit to the influence of the Christian home.

We have to be salt and light to the world around us in this arena. Healthy families that are intentional breed healthy families!

When parents have godly character and wisdom for raising children, they produce a family that reflects the love and integrity of Christ. If children grow up seeing one standard in church and another at home, they tend to rebel against standards altogether.

Family should be lived out together.

6. Government

This mountain is important, and that being said, we must be willing to do what Jesus did in Luke 2:52 (write it down):

_____

_____

_____

The government needs the Kingdom influence to aid it in finding kingdom solutions to this decaying system we are in. People instinctively want to be governed by people who are honest and righteous.

Write Proverbs 11:10:

_____

_____

_____

People want leaders who are not self-serving, but who actually govern sacrificially for the benefit of the whole. Jesus modeled this perfectly. He served like a king, and ruled like a servant. We need to do the same.

Why do we need to conquer this mountain? Because two of the most basic roles of government are to create a realm of safety and a realm of prosperity. Those are at their truest and most effective when they come from the Kingdom mindset of the Scriptures!

7. <u>Science and Medicine</u>

Disease is on the increase. For generations the Church has been hidden behind false piety that medicine is of the devil. This is simply not true! When the body has a dysfunction, and someone is diagnosed with anxiety or panic disorders, the Church tells them they need to just pray and resist the urge to take "medicine". But if their eyes go bad, they get glasses. There is no difference! Using science and medicine as a secondary option to divine healing is not a sin. God created all good things!

Write James 1: 17:

_____

_____

_____

_____

If it comes from God, it's good.

We, as the church should pray at every meeting for those in this field. For doctors, nurses, ambulance workers, hospital employees, police, firefighters and more. We should pray that the righteous be assigned to these places of influence. Our goal should be to make it nearly impossible to go to hell from our city.

Real love has few opponents. When we go in humbly to share love in this arena, you will hardly ever be denied.

So how do we invade these mountains?

First, we take territory from Satan in the place of prayer, with the power of the Holy Spirit, through the mighty weapons available to us. We know spiritual warfare involves pulling down strongholds of false reasoning. We pray against the enemy's influence on whatever area we are aware. Our prayers should be specific. Listening to Holy Spirit in our minds, He will tell us how to pray.

Secondly, after we pray for a specific sphere of influence, be it government, schools, media, or whatever it is, He may call us to penetrate that influential place for Him. Placing us, like Daniel or Joseph, in a place of authority.

Question: Who were the people groups that the Apostle Paul was assigned to reach in the book of Acts? _____

Think it over and don't skip this. I want you to see this.

To whom was Paul sent to preach to?

_____

Was it the Gentiles? Or the Jews? Was it both? Was it neither? _____

Look at Acts 9:15 (write it down):

_____

_____

_____

_____

You see that Paul was sent to the Gentiles AND the Jews, but ALSO to another people group...

The Kings

Who are modern day Kings? They are the ones who occupy the high places, the spheres of influence in the seven mountains of culture. They write the songs you sing and make the movies you watch! They tell you what's in fashion and what's out of fashion.

Read Luke 4:5-6.

Notice that the devil did not create the kingdoms of this world. He says to Jesus, "All this has been delivered to me, and I give it to whomever I wish." That means that the kingdoms were made for humanity. And that they have the capacity to reveal the glory of the One who called them into being.

We may not realize this, but each of these mountains is spiritual mountains. If we take serious our role to invade them, and do the necessary preparations, we can inherit them.

That means that some of you are called to the music and entertainment industry, NOT TO SING THEIR SONGS, but to bring the glory of the Kingdom of God into that mountain of influence

Some of you are called to be doctors, or nurses, or medical students, and your willingness to prepare will position you to find cures that secularized culture cannot find. Cures to diseases, cancer, and the like.

Some of you are called to be teachers who teach with moral excellence, not just give information

We cannot hide behind the walls of the church and expect the world to come to us.

Matthew 10:16 (write it down):

_____

_____

_____

_____

He's not sending the wolves to us; He's sending us to them. We cannot go blindly! That's laziness and a false understanding of grace! We must prepare! We must educate! We must pray!

The fact is that the church lacks cultural power because it focuses on changing the world from within the Church mountain rather than releasing the Church into the marketplace to all seven mountains.

Isaiah 2:2 (Write this prophetic word down):

_____

_____

_____

_____

_____

_____

_____

If we are going to do more than the generations before us that screamed at the darkness, we must take this mandate serious to invade darkness with marvelous light.

Read Acts 28:7-10

Read it

Seriously, stop now and read it

When Paul, a political prisoner, healed an island chief's father after the shipwreck, he was given an immediate upgrade of authority on the island! We carry something as kings and priests that is powerful.

It is a combining anointing! As kings we have authority to administrate over earth and ALL demonic activity. As priests we have power to access heavenly places in Christ!

We are salt. We are intended to slow the decay of the culture!

We have to stop living for the day only, and start seeing what God sees, and investing in that. Giving is a command from Jesus, it is not optional.

Matthew 6:1-2 NLT

2   <u>When you give</u> to someone in need......

That's not just money, that's giving your attention, and planning, and sacrifices to God's plan for your life's influence! God's plan is not that you have a poverty spirit. A poverty spirit always feels like their resources are limited. God never intended for us to live in poverty in any area of our lives. But he does want us to be good stewards over what he has given us, so he won't be wasting good seed on us because we're not responsible.

Psalm 37:25 (write it down):

_____

_____

_____

_____

_____

"The doorway to breaking the spirit of poverty is giving" – Karen Wheaton

Genesis 13:2 (write it down):

_____

_____

_____

What we love about tithing is that it is specific and proportionate to our income; we know how much we "have" to give. Which, ironically, is the same thing we hate about giving. That it is NOT proportionate to our income; it is out of our heart's overflow, and our good stewardship that we are permitted to give more, and more. And that scares us because we love our money going to us...

"It is possible to give without loving, but it is impossible to truly love, without giving." This is not just about money. This is about breaking the poverty mentality! This is about breaking the mindset that you just "go to church" on the weekends as an addendum to your week.

What are you passionate about??
_____

What are you called to do???
_____

What excuse are you using because it's not "churchy" enough to be of God?
_____
_____
_____

What plans are you establishing after this week is over to continue to grow, and to invade this Babylonian society with your Kingdom tools?

_____

_____

_____

_____

_____

_____

_____

_____

_____

_____

_____

_____

_____

_____

Additional notes:

If you have any questions, or you would like to receive prayer or advice for something, please do not hesitate to contact us.

I pray this workbook has sparked a fire in you, and you begin this amazing walk of true commitment.

If you would like to receive Sermon CD's and newsletters concerning the revival movement at Addereth Church, simply go to our website, and sign up for partnership!

www.addereth.com

Or call us at 706.992.2322